Prince George Public Library
888 Canada Games Way
Prince George, BC V2L 5T6
250-563-9251

December -- 2020

CHOOSING YOUR COSTUME IN *FORTNITE*®

SHARON CHRISCOE

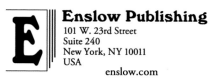

Enslow Publishing
101 W. 23rd Street
Suite 240
New York, NY 10011
USA
enslow.com

Published in 2020 by Enslow Publishing, LLC
101 W. 23rd Street, Suite 240, New York, NY 10011

Library of Congress Cataloging-in-Publication Data
Names: Chriscoe, Sharon.
Title: Choosing your costume in Fortnite® / Sharon Chriscoe.
Description: New York : Enslow Publishing, 2020. | Series: The unofficial
Fortnite® survival guide | Includes glossary and index.
Identifiers: ISBN 9781978517110 (pbk.) | ISBN 9781978517134
(library bound) | ISBN 9781978517127 (6 pack)
Subjects: LCSH: Fortnite Battle Royale (Game)--Juvenile literature. | Imaginary
wars and battles--Juvenile literature. | Video games--Juvenile literature.
Classification: LCC GV1469.35.F67 C57 2020 | DDC 794.8--dc23

Fortnite is a trademark of Epic Games, and its use in this book does not
imply a recommendation or endorsement of this title by Epic Games.

Printed in the United States of America

To Our Readers: We have done our best to make sure all website addresses in this book
were active and appropriate when we went to press. However, the author and the publisher
have no control over and assume no liability for the material available on those websites
or on any websites they may link to. Any comments or suggestions can be sent by email to
customerservice@enslow.com.

CONTENTS

INTRODUCTION

Costumes have a long history of helping people disguise themselves as someone different. For centuries, people have donned costumes and taken the stage as Romeo or Juliet, Faust, or Cyrano de Bergerac. These days, peo-

ple dress up for Halloween. Some dress up for Mardi Gras, the historic festival that falls before Lent each year. Others attend fan conventions dressed as their favorite heroic characters, like Superman, Wonder Woman, or Spider-Man—or their favorite villains such as the Joker, Darth Vader, Thanos, or Red Skull. Costumes can be a lot of fun!

Costumes, or skins, are also fun in *Fortnite*, the game released in 2017 that has taken the world by storm. *Fortnite* can be played in three different modes: Save the World, a survival mode in which players fight off hordes of zombie-like husks using weapons, traps, and well-planned fortifications. *Fortnite* Creative

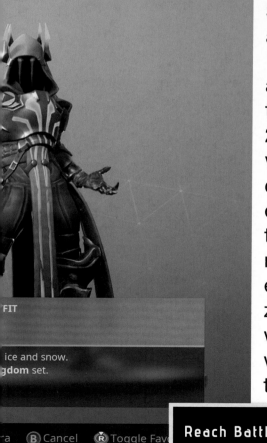

FIT

ice and snow.
gdom set.

a B Cancel R Toggle Fav

Reach Battle Pass Tier 100 and unlock the power of The Ice King skin! Players can unlock new colors, too.

is a sandbox mode that allows players to build and explore without danger of attacks. And finally, there's *Fortnite:* Battle Royale, in which players engage in a fight to the death against up to one hundred opponents. The last survivor wins the coveted Victory Royale. Skins are particularly important to game strategy in *Fortnite:* Battle Royale. You can choose from numerous skins, which can make your avatar look cool, adorable, or intimidating. Skins can be purchased with in-game currency called V-Bucks, unlocked over time, or through earning rewards. In Save the World, you can unlock additional skins by completing certain missions.

Some skins offer different advantages. Others are just plain creepy, cute, or hilarious and might distract another player long enough for you to get away, hide, or follow through with a game-winning strategy. Let's take a closer look at some of the skins offered in *Fortnite*, how you can acquire them, and how to develop your own game strategy around the costume you choose.

CHAPTER 1

Your Costume Has Plenty to Say

When a character dons a new skin, he or she isn't just in a new disguise, that character takes on the characteristics of that skin. Skins can't literally speak, but they can still say a lot. Scary costumes can strike fear in another player. Silly costumes can lead to laughter. Adorably sweet costumes can make

GET YOUR SKIN ON!

Each *Fortnite* skin is assigned a rarity. Each rarity is labeled under one of these five different types: Common, Uncommon, Rare, Epic, and Legendary. The rarer the skin is, the more valuable it is.

EDITING

OUTFIT

FILTER - ALL

LT ∞ ! RT

Ⓧ **EDIT STYLE**   Ⓐ **SAVE AND EXIT**

Hold to chat

What are you in the mood to say with your *Fornite* skin? The Peely skin makes your avatar into a human banana.

people smile. When choosing a skin in *Fortnite*, bear in mind that your skin will have plenty to say about you as a player.

era   ⒷCancel   ⓇToggle Favorite

Be One with Your Skin

In battle, your *Fortnite* skin gives your opponents the first impression of who you are and what you're capable of doing. Really digging in and becoming the character of your skin can have a powerful effect on your game.

By simply changing your outward appearance through different skins, your inner personality may change as well. A study published in the *Journal of Sport and Exercise Psychology* found that exercising in red workout clothes increased heart rates and gave extra weight bearing strength in comparison to those exercising in a different color.

This could indicate why you may feel stealthy while playing *Fortnite* in a Ninja Class skin. Or why you feel extra brave while wearing a Soldier Class skin.

Accessorize That Skin!

Players aren't the only ones who wear skins in *Fortnite*. Your Harvesting Tool also has them! Just like many people who enjoy sprucing up their winter coat with a decorative scarf, many players find it fun to add a little style to their Pickaxes. The Harvesting Tool skins don't alter your Pickaxe's performance or efficiency, but they do look really cool. Sometimes they can even be quite festive, like the Snow Globe Pickaxe skin, which is decked out with a gingerbread man inside, nutcracker soldier uniform-like decals, and topped with a black hat.

Legendary | Hero
CLOAKED SHADOW
✳ Ninja

⚡ 58 ★★★★★ LV 20 / 20

Health **3,556**   Shield **1,737**

Health	3,556
Health Regen Rate	87
Shield	1,737
Shield Regen Rate	425
Shield Regen Delay	8
Hero Ability Damage	4.3
Hero Healing Modifier	4.27
Run Speed	410
Sprint Speed	550

Lv 92   130

ties   Perks

LB RB

agon Slash
st: 50 energy
oldown: 10 seconds
sh forward, slashing
emies for 904.1 damage.

rowing Stars
st: 30 energy
oldown: 10 seconds
leash a volley of
owing stars, which deal
4.0 damage.

oke Bomb
st: 40 energy
oldown: 45 seconds
op a smoke bomb which
ws enemies and deals
3.8 damage per second.

Cheer is jolly.

23,867 / 6,250

Y View Evolution

Hold to chat   View   R Toggle Favorite   B Back

Epic-rarity skin Cloaked Shadow's shadowy wings and reindeer-like horns are ready to wreak havoc.

In *Fortnite*, as in the real world, there are different levels of accessories. While some scarves might come with the purchase of a

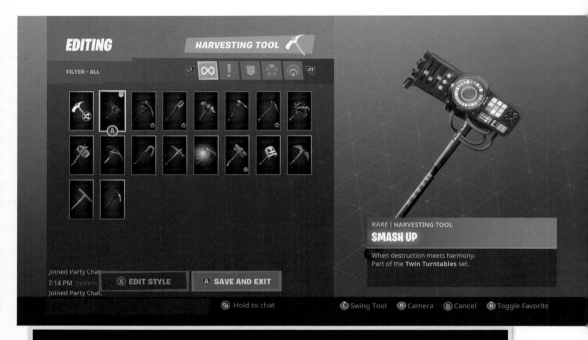

EDITING

HARVESTING TOOL

FILTER - ALL

RARE | HARVESTING TOOL
SMASH UP

When destruction meets harmony.
Part of the **Twin Turntables** set.

Joined Party Chat
7:14 PM System
Joined Party Chat

Ⓧ EDIT STYLE   Ⓐ SAVE AND EXIT

Hold to chat   Swing Tool   Camera   Cancel   Toggle Favorite

Your Pickaxe can dress up, too! The Smash Up Harvesting
Tool skin lets your tool double as a turntable.

coat, others may cost big bucks. In *Fortnite*, upgrading is the way in which you earn by gaining points while unlocking achievements or going on missions. It's important to keep in mind that if you return to a lower level's playing area, your Pickaxe will downgrade to that level.

CHAPTER 2

Feel Your Best, Play Your Best

Developing a strategy is key to playing *Fortnite*. If you're a stealth player who hides out until the smoke clears, your best strategy might include a really effective camouflage. You won't want, for example, to hide in a small bush wearing a bulky Tomatohead or Toxic Trooper skin. Jungle Scout or Devastator would bring you a lot more success.

Choosing a Skin

Every avatar comes with a default skin, assigned randomly by the game. You can

It's often hard for snipers to target your avatar's real head inside the giant Tomatohead skin.

CHANGE YOUR SKIN!

So, you've decided you aren't happy with your current skin. Not a problem! Changing your skin is quick and easy. Simply go to the Locker tab on the menu, click the Outfits tab, select the skin you want to change to, pay for your skin using V-Bucks, and you're on your way!

play using that skin, enroll in Battle Pass and wait and unlock new skins, or buy a different one using V-Bucks. It can be fun to try out different skins and see which ones you like best. Once you have several skins, you can pick out whichever one suits your mood that day before the match begins.

Colorful Costumes Rock!

Don't just wear your *Fortnite* costume . . . feel it! Color can change your mood or how you play. Wearing red is known to give energy and gain attention. Wearing yellow can bring

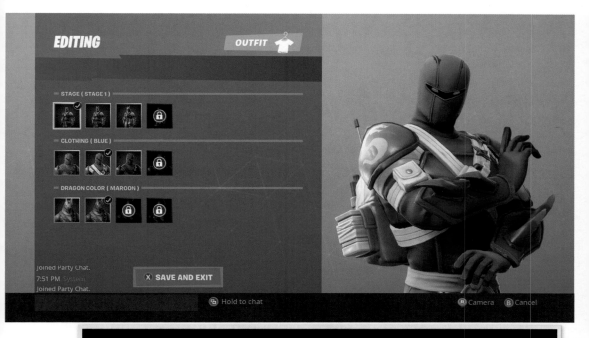

EDITING

OUTFIT

STAGE (STAGE 1)

CLOTHING (BLUE)

DRAGON COLOR (MAROON)

Joined Party Chat.
7:51 PM System
Joined Party Chat.

X SAVE AND EXIT

Hold to chat   R Camera   B Cancel

This Hybrid ninja's default skin color is red, but by completing weekly challenges, you can unlock new colors.

cheerfulness and happiness. And both green and blue have a natural calming effect to them. The next time you're in the middle of a game and you're just not feeling it, try changing your *Fortnite* skin and see if the new shade gives you a fresh burst of energy.

But be sure to check your V-Bucks balance and the rarity level of the skin you want because the rarer the skin is, the more V-Bucks it's going to cost.

CHAPTER 3

What's Your Number?

Do you always pick the same number for your *Fortnite* skin? Does your favorite number say something about you? Some studies say yes! In fact, there's even a chart for numbers and their meanings. But remember the chart is purely for fun.

The Evolution of Numbers

The number zero wasn't always a number. Thousands of years ago, many people had difficulties understanding how you could count something that wasn't there. Eventually, zero gained its spot on the number grid as a placeholder.

In sports, numbers might represent what position a player plays. They also serve as identifiers and make it easier to find one

LeBron James of the LA Lakers sports his lucky number 23 jersey, which was once Michael Jordan's number.

player on a field full of athletes wearing the same uniforms.

If you've always wanted to play like your favorite athlete, choose a sports *Fortnite* skin, choose your team colors and logo, add your favorite player's number to your skin, and have fun!

FORTNITE EQUALS A FORTNIGHT!

Fortnite soccer skins have a default number of fourteen because the name *Fortnite* is derived from *fortnight*, the term used to mean a period of fourteen days. But don't worry! If the number fourteen isn't your favorite, you can always change it.

RARE | OUTFIT

SUPER STRIKER

Represent your country in style!
Part of the **Goalbound** set.
[*Selectable Styles*]

1,200

X GET V-BUCKS

A PREVIEW STYLES

Y Buy As A Gift

2FA required to send gifts

Joined Party Chat.
8:07 PM
Joined Party Chat.

Hold to chat   R Camera   B Back

Pick your colors, nation, and favorite number in this rare customizable Goalbound skin.

Luck of the Numbers

With seven days in a week, seven colors in the rainbow, seven continents on Earth, and even seven notes on a musical scale, it's no wonder that many people consider seven a lucky number.

On the opposite side is the unlucky number thirteen. Many people fear it so much that some buildings skip the number thirteen on their floors, and people won't get married or buy a house on the thirteenth of the month. Even the number thirteen tarot card is named Death!

However, neither the number seven nor the number thirteen have proven themselves to be lucky or unlucky. But that doesn't stop *Fortnite* players who believe in luck from choosing their favorite lucky number for their sports skins!

Don't fear the Death Card! This tarot card doesn't indicate death in your near future; it simply implies a change is on its way.

FEAR THIRTEEN!

Triskaidekaphobia may be a very long word, but it has a simple explanation as to why it's used to describe people's fear of the number thirteen. "Tris" means *three*. "Kai" means *and*. "Deka" means *ten*. And "phobia" means *fear*. Put that all together and you have "fear thirteen!"

Does that mean if a *Fortnite* player chooses the number thirteen as his or her skin, that player is telling opponents to fear him or her? Maybe so! It might be part of that player's game strategy.

Some kinds of fear in *Fortnite*, like in any online activity, can be a healthy kind of fear that keeps players out of real-life danger. Remember to always follow online safety rules: never share your personal information, such as your real name, your address, your phone number, your school, or any other details that would make it possible for an online predator to become a real-life danger. Keep your information private, stay safe, and have fun!

CHAPTER 4

In It to Win It

B eginner *Fortnite* players may think using their default skin is a disadvantage compared to more seasoned player's skins, but that's not true. The green-and-brown basic skin is perfect for hiding behind a tree or in a bush, which may be just what a beginner needs in order to get the upper hand against his or her opponent.

Hiding in Plain Sight

Camouflaging is a simple yet very effective tactic for both humans and animals. If your enemy doesn't see you, he or she won't attack you. Animals in the wild use this tactic for survival. Since being introduced by the French Army in 1915, military camouflaging has helped soldiers defeat their enemies. And some clever *Fortnite* players have been known to choose

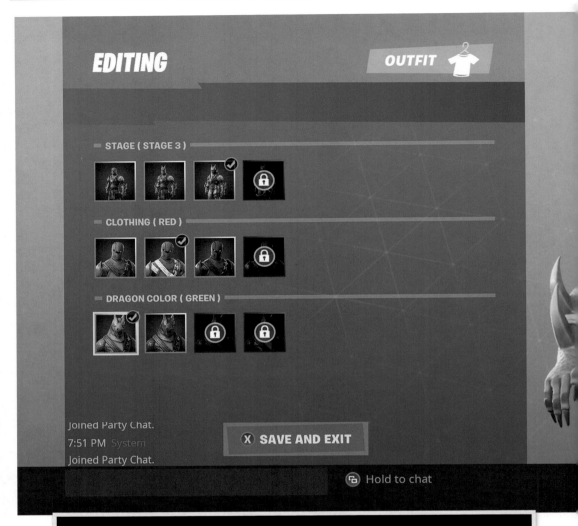

EDITING

OUTFIT

STAGE (STAGE 3)

CLOTHING (RED)

DRAGON COLOR (GREEN)

Joined Party Chat.
7:51 PM System
Joined Party Chat.

(X) SAVE AND EXIT

Hold to chat

Be one with your surroundings. Look around, change your skin's color for camouflage, and then hide in plain sight.

their skins based upon their surroundings so they can stand in the middle of a battlefield without being detected.

Disruptive Behavior Is Sometimes a Good Thing!

Ⓡ Camera   Ⓑ Cancel

Fortnite players can learn defense mechanisms from animals surviving in the wild. A zebra's bold stripes when a group is herded together appear to predators as a disruptive massive maze of black and white. Not even a powerful lion will attack when there's no way to tell where one zebra ends and another begins!

This same tactic can be used by *Fortnite* players in squad mode by creating confusion when the entire squad wears the same skin. Hopefully this will lead to them being the last team standing!

AS COOL AS A STATUE!

With its stone wings and concrete appearance, *Fortnite*'s Love Ranger skin could come in quite handy if you find yourself in battle at a cemetery. Imagine standing as still as a statue and conquering with a sneak attack!

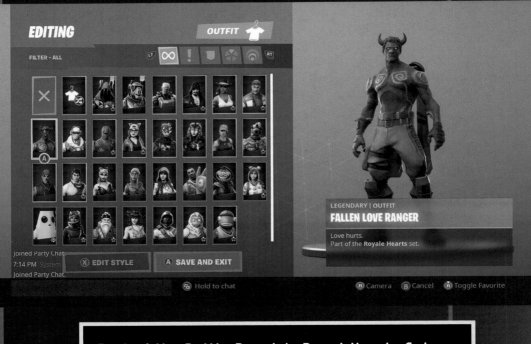

EDITING

OUTFIT

FILTER - ALL

LEGENDARY | OUTFIT
FALLEN LOVE RANGER

Love hurts.
Part of the **Royale Hearts** set.

Joined Party Chat
7:14 PM System
Joined Party Chat

Ⓧ EDIT STYLE   Ⓐ SAVE AND EXIT

Hold to chat   Ⓡ Camera   Ⓑ Cancel   Ⓡ Toggle Favorite

Part of the Battle Royale's Royal Hearts Set, The Fallen Love Ranger resembles cupid and features concrete-like skin and stone wings.

Psychology in Combat

The mind is a powerful thing! What you feel often trickles down to how you react. If you find yourself in battle against a more seasoned *Fortnite* player, try hopping around in the Bunny Brawler skin or opt to showcase the big, frightening smile of Ginger Gunner. These skins create gut reactions, which will hopefully give you the upper hand in combat.

Get comfy in your favorite seat and get ready to gear up for *Fortnite*!

25

FEAR ME!

Fortnite's Legendary Reaper skin resembles hired hit man John Wick and packs a hand cannon. That's not a weapon any player wants to go up against!

Fortnite's Legendary Elite Agent skin is available only once a player reaches Tier 87. This tier is only reached by savvy, slick, and skillful players.

Fear is one of the greatest distractions on Earth. It has been known to cause people to freeze, use poor judgment, and even surrender. Make your opponent fear you and claim your victory!

GLOSSARY

CAMOUFLAGING Altering one's appearance for concealment, usually by changing to match a background color for hiding in plain sight.

DEFAULT A selection that is made automatically, but can often be changed later on.

DERIVES Comes from.

DISADVANTAGE A less favorable position.

HARVESTING TOOL A *Fortnite* Pickaxe, used to collect building materials and other items.

MECHANISMS Capabilities to do something.

MODE A function for how something is done.

MOODS State of how someone is feeling.

PREDATORS Animals or people who attack vulnerable prey.

RARITY Something unusual.

SEASONED Experienced.

SKIN The name for your costume in *Fortnite*.

SQUAD A team of four that plays together.

STEALTHY Being quiet and cautious, hiding and moving around in a sneaky manner in order to not be seen.

TAROT Cards used by fortune tellers to predict someone's future.

TIER 87 An extremely high game layer that only experienced players reach.

UPGRADING Improving something by adding or replacing.

V-BUCKS Money that is used for purchasing items; short for Vindertech Bucks.

VILLAINS Bad characters who do evil things.

FOR MORE INFORMATION

Charity Gaming
Website: http://www.charity-gaming.org

Entertainment Software Association of Canada (ESAC)
Website: http://theesa.ca

Esports Foundation, Inc.
Website: https://esports.us

Games for Change
Website: http://www.gamesforchange.org

IndyPopCon
Website: https://indypopcon.com

International Game Developers Association (IGDA)
Website: https://www.igda.org

FOR FURTHER READING

Ashby, Stephen. *Ready, Set, Play!* New York, NY: Scholastic, 2017.

Brady, Dustin, and Jesse Brady. *Trapped in a Video Game: The Invisible Invasion*. Kansas City, MO: Andrews McMeel Publishing, 2018.

Cunningham, Kevin. *Video Game Designer*. Ann Arbor, MI: Cherry Lake Publishing, 2016.

Gifford, Clive. *Gaming Record Breakers*. London, United Kingdom: Carlton Books Limited, 2016.

Gregory, Josh. *Fortnite Skins.* Ann Arbor, MI: Cherry Lake Publishing, 2019.

Krensky, Stephen, and Scott Burroughs. *History of Fun Stuff: The High Score and Lowdown on Video Games*. New York, NY: Simon Spotlight, 2015.

Nakaya, Andrea C. *Video Games and Youth*. San Diego, CA: ReferencePoint Press, Inc., 2015.

Paris, David, and Stephanie Herweck Paris. *History of Video Games* (TIME FOR KIDS® Nonfiction Readers). Huntington Beach, CA: Teacher Created Materials, 2017.

Rosenburg, Kenneth. *STEAM Jobs in Game Development.* Vero Beach, FL: Rourke Educational Media, 2017.

Slingerland, Janet. *Video Game Coding*. Lake Elmo, MN: Focus Readers, 2019.

INDEX

About the Author

Sharon Chriscoe writes for children of all ages. From picture books for the very young to novels for upper middle grade readers, she is passionate about creating lively worlds for children to grow and learn in. She is the author of numerous books for Running Press Kids. She and her husband live in North Carolina and have three children and one grandchild.

Photo Credits

Cover © iStockphoto.com/Studia72; p. 13 ESPAT Media/Getty Images; p. 17 Robert Laberge/Getty Images; p. 19 Petchjira/iStock/Getty Images; p. 25 PBWPIX/Alamy Stock Photo.

Design and Layout: Brian Garvey; Editor: Bethany Bryan;
Photo Researcher: Nicole DiMella
Fortnite consultant: Sam Keppeler